Tasting

A Troll Question Book™

By Kathie Billingslea Smith & Victoria Crenson
Illustrated by Robert S. Storms
Medical Consultant: Ira T. Fine, M.D.

Library of Congress Cataloging in Publication Data

Smith, Kathie Billingslea.
  Tasting.

  (A Troll question book)
  Summary: Uses a question and answer format to explain our sense of taste.
  1. Taste—Juvenile literature. [1. Taste.
2. Senses and sensation.. 3. Questions and answers]
I. Crenson, Victoria. II. Storms, Robert S., ill.
III. Title.
QP456.S65   1988   612'.87   87-5884
ISBN 0-8167-1014-7 (lib. bdg.)
ISBN 0-8167-1015-5 (pbk.)

Troll Associates
Mahwah, N.J.

How do I taste

The brain and the tongue work together to help you taste food.

Stand in front of a mirror and look at your tongue. It is covered with many tiny bumps. These bumps contain *taste buds*, the organs for tasting. There are thousands of these taste buds in your mouth.

food?

Let's say you bite into a strawberry. *Receptor cells* in the taste buds send messages along special nerves to the brain. The brain compares that message to all the different tastes in its taste memory "library." The brain says, "*Mmmmm . . . delicious strawberry. That's it!*"

This does not always happen

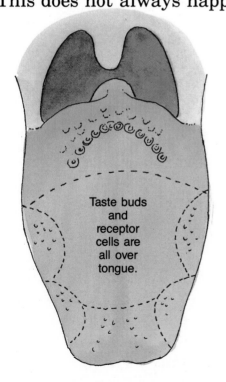

Taste buds and receptor cells are all over tongue.

quickly. Sometimes it takes several seconds for the taste receptors to send a message and for the brain to recognize a flavor. Seeing and smelling a food can help the brain decide what you are tasting more quickly.

How do my eyes and

The sense of taste is the weakest of all the senses. To help you taste and enjoy food the brain needs clues from the eyes and the nose.

Suppose there is a glass of juice on a table. The eyes tell the brain that the juice is purple. "Grape juice is purple," says the brain.

The nose smells the purple drink, and another clue goes to the brain — smells like grapes!

Take a sip. The taste buds on the tongue send the final clue. This purple juice that smells like grapes is cool and sweet and tastes just like . . . GRAPES!

nose help me taste?

Sometime, just for fun, blindfold yourself and hold your nose while eating. It will be hard to tell the difference between similar foods like Swiss cheese and American cheese.

When you have a cold and your nose is stuffed up, everything seems to taste the same. Then your nose cannot help you enjoy food. The sense of taste alone is not very strong.

How many different

Your tongue can tell four tastes without the help of your nose: sweet, sour, salty, and bitter. Special taste buds for each one of them are grouped in separate places on your tongue.

The taste buds on the tip of the tongue taste *sweet* foods. That is why people like to lick ice-cream cones. Taste buds for *salt* are along the sides of the front of the tongue. *Sour* tastes can be measured farther back along the sides. *Bitter* foods can best be tasted on the back of the tongue.

Take out a sugar lump, a dill pickle, a potato chip, and an orange peel. See which part of the tongue helps you taste each food the best.

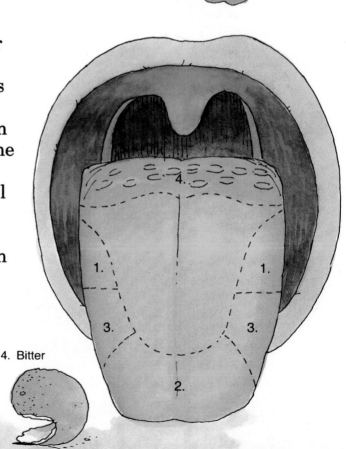

1. Sour

2. Sweet

3. Salty

4. Bitter

flavors can I taste?

Most food flavors are combinations of these tastes.

Taste buds work together to help you recognize these blended flavors. Lemon meringue pie is both sour and sweet. Iced tea is sweet, sour, and bitter at the same time. Everything that you eat or drink has a special flavor of its own. That is one reason why eating is fun!

What gives a food

The taste, smell, temperature, and texture of a food all combine to give it a special flavor. Vanilla ice cream is cold, smooth, and sweet. Many apples are juicy, tart, and crisp. Potato chips are salty, dry, and crunchy. A soggy potato chip just doesn't taste right!

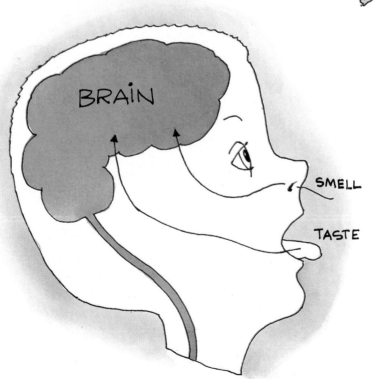

BRAIN

SMELL

TASTE

To recognize a flavor and let you enjoy it, the brain needs information from your nose and tongue. There are two different kinds of nerves that carry messages from the tongue to the brain. One kind sends information just about taste. The other kind of nerve sends messages about temperature and "feel."

its flavor?

Close your eyes while you eat a peanut butter and jelly sandwich. Your nose is smelling the aroma and telling your brain about it. Your tongue sends messages about the taste, temperature, and texture of what you are eating. By mingling these messages your brain decides that this is crunchy-style peanut butter and grape jelly on whole wheat bread. Now for a sip of cold milk!

Why do I like some foods

Everyone has certain foods that they especially like to eat. But one person's favorite food may be on another person's "I hate to eat" list! Some people like liver. Other folks can't stand the taste of it. Many people think that olives taste great, but some others will never eat them. No one knows for sure why this is true.

People usually enjoy eating most of the foods that their family eats. If your family likes lasagna or watermelon or chocolate chip cookies, then you probably do, too.

better than others?

But people in different parts of the world do not necessarily like the same foods you do. In Japan people like to eat *sushi,* which is raw fish wrapped in seaweed. Many Russians enjoy cold beet soup on a warm day. Children in Mexico eat food that is so spicy it might make your eyes water! If you are accustomed to these foods, you probably think that they taste good, too.

Make a menu of your favorite meal.
Ask a friend to make one, too. When you compare menus, they will probably be different. Different people like to eat different foods.

Perhaps try tasting a food you've never tried before. Give it a chance. You might like it!

Why does my mouth smell certain

Glands in the mouth give off a watery fluid called *saliva*. A certain amount of it is always flowing. This keeps the mouth moist and comfortable.

When you see or smell a food you like, your eyes or nose send a message to your brain. The brain thinks that you are going to eat the food. It tells the glands in your mouth to start

water when I see or foods?

giving off saliva. This helps to dissolve the chemicals in food so that your taste buds can taste the flavor.

Your body gets ready to eat even though you haven't taken a bite yet! And this sometimes happens when you just think about a favorite food!

Even though the salivary glands are busy, the mouth and throat often dry out. Breathing, talking, and eating dry or salty foods can make the mouth feel dry. Sometimes a sip of water or juice moistens the mouth and you feel comfortable again.

But, at other times, you need a *big* drink. Why? Well, a large

thirsty?

portion of the body is fluid. You need water every day to stay alive. When special receptors spot a water shortage in the body, they signal the brain. "DRINK!" says the brain. Then there is nothing like the taste of a tall glass of cold water!

As the body's water level goes back to normal, your brain turns off the thirst message and you feel much better.

Exercising can make you thirsty. During hard exercise the body loses water through the skin by sweating. To replace the water their bodies lose, long-distance runners take short drinks during races.

Why do hot peppers

Foods that are made with chili or jalapeño peppers, or certain mustards and spices are called "hot" foods. They do not feel hot when you touch them with your fingers. But one bite of a jalapeño pepper will make your mouth feel like it is on fire! *Yowww!*

When you eat these kinds of foods, they react with your taste buds so that you can taste them. But they also react with pain receptors that are in the mouth.

make my mouth burn?

Special messages of pain are sent to the brain. That is what makes your mouth feel like it is burning.

In southern India, where the climate is hot, people eat very "hot" foods called *curries*. The Indians say that eating curries makes a person perspire. Perspiration helps keep the body cool.

How do animals use

Animals use their sense of taste to find food to eat. Most plant-eating animals like to eat sweet foods. They do not like foods with a bitter taste. Scientists think that this is one way that animals' tastes protect them. Sweet-tasting plants and fruits are usually safe to eat. But poisonous berries and plants often taste bitter. The bad tastes act as a warning to say,
"Don't eat me!"

P-TEWY!

A bad taste protects some animals from being eaten. For example, birds and other insect eaters that try to eat monarch butterflies learn quickly that they taste terrible and leave them alone. Many toads give off a bitter flavor when they are frightened. One taste of a toad and an animal will spit him out and look somewhere else for supper.

their sense of taste?

A keen sense of taste for sweetness helps some animals find food. Bees, houseflies, butterflies, and minnows can taste very tiny amounts of sugar.

Cats, on the other hand, cannot taste sweetness at all. But they love salt. That is why they like to lick the salty perspiration on your skin. Their tongues feel just like scratchy sandpaper!

Catfish enjoy eating just about anything. But koalas eat only one food — eucalyptus leaves. This makes koalas smell like cough drops.

How do animals use

Of course, many animals use their tongues to taste food. Cows, elephants, dogs, birds,

scoop up groups of ants. Bees use their tongues like straws to half suck, half lick nectar from flowers.

horses, and lions all taste with their tongues.

But a few animals have special ways to use their tongues. For instance, frogs have long, sticky tongues that they poke out to snare insects that are flying by. Anteaters use their long, sticky tongues to

heir tongues?

Some animals do not use their tongues to taste at all. They use other body parts to taste food. Butterflies taste with their feet! Catfish taste food with their whole bodies — their fins, their feelers, and even their tails!

What happens when

If a sip of hot chocolate burns your tongue, it hurts! The hot liquid stimulates temperature and pain receptors on the tongue. The receptors send a message to the brain — *Ouch!*

Sometimes the burn is bad enough to "knock out" some of the taste buds on the tongue. For a while, you cannot taste very well at all. But taste buds replace themselves very quickly.

burn my tongue?

New taste buds replace old ones every ten to thirty hours.

Remember that an ice cube in a cup of hot chocolate or a bowl of hot soup will cool it down quickly and keep you from burning your tongue.

Does my sense of taste change as I grow older?

When you were a baby, you could taste foods very well. You had taste buds on your tongue, inside your cheeks, and on the roof of your mouth! You had more taste buds than you do now.

As you grow older, the taste buds on the sides and roof of your mouth disappear. But the ones on your tongue remain.

When you grow up and become very old, many of the taste buds on your tongue lose their ability to replace themselves. Then you will not be able to taste food as clearly as you once could. Sometimes elderly people have poor appetites because of this problem.